1

Power of focus

HOW TO DEFEAT LAZINESS AND ACHIEVE

YOUR GOAL

Would you like to know how to accomplished anything in life?Would you like to make your dream any dream come true?
Would you like to achieve huge

financial success and become the 1% Rich kids on the block? New information contain in this

book will show you how to get anything you want in life. Read on.

ATTENTION TO THE READER

While the scholars of this book have endeavored sensible undertakings to ensure the accuracy of the information contained in this book, the author and distributer anticipate no responsibility as to disasteror lost that happened in your life, nor changes to be made on any information contained in this, and therefore , the author deny all assurances, whether imparted or recommended, with regards to the precision or

CHAPTER GUIDE

CHAPTER 1   CREATE GOALS EVERYDAY

I 'M PLANNING TO WRITE ANOTHER
EBOOK ABOUT OUR BRAIN
REGARDING
FOCUS .IF YOU WOULD LIKE A FREE
COPY OF IT ,PLEASE REPLY TO MY

EMAIL ADDRESS: vikpeter83@gmail.com

ON THE SUBJECT,WRITE: "I WANT
THE FREE EBOOK"JUST MAKE SURE
TO PUT MY EMAIL ADDRESS
ON YOUR CONTACT LIST SO
THE EBOOK WON'T END UP IN
YOUR SPAM.

CREATE GOALS EVERYDAY

You're occupied daily. I'm occupied daily . Everybody's occupied daily .

However despite this busy occupied time everyday , we frequently don't
feel particularly "efficient" use of our time everyday. Whole weeks can streak
by abruptly by good-for-nothing sms messages, meetings, and administrative
undertakings while the "gigantic stuff" is left undone. As the nineteenth-century
logician Henry David Thoreau said, "It isn't sufficient to be occupied with a certain
task or work . So are the ants. The question is : What task or work are we
occupied about?"

If we desire to reclaim control of our workday calendars and essential task needs,
the easiest method to do it is by method of steadily and constantly thinking how
we're investing our energy and time. In any case, When we are busy , what questions
should we ask ? I contacted a bunch of typical 99U people and the 99U tradition
sound framework to get their bits-of-knowledge on day by day task control.

This is what they stated :

From Leo Babauta of Zen conduct:

What are you doing at this point in time?

The direct action of being more mindful of what you're occupied with at this very
 moment , causes you to perceive what you are really supposed to do –
 developing something unprecedented, completing the major goal. Time after time,
we get diverted in immaterial or immature undertakings –
returning to the present
regularly, will certainly help in your focus on the only important work that matters.

From Tony Schwartz of the quality task:

Are you booking time every day to have mindfulness without interference?

Put aside one period for the duration of the day – close to a hour and a half at any given moment – to have mindfulness without intrusion. Time, at the end of the day, to accomplish something basic, but not important – to carefully record something, repeat, strategize, consider, paint on , on a long haul venture.

The key here is control of awareness. We're so distracted, and we're bolstering that inclination to be distracted on each event, that we constantly switch between our daily goals. We have to re- learn our focus, daily . Concentrated interest can serve commitments – that is the left half of the brain at work, doing sane, deductive, coherent, advance by utilizing step by step addressing.

The other kind of focus, which involves being inventive, is where the right brain is prevailing. That calls for profoundly calming the thinking. It was Betty Edwards(drawing on the best possible part of the brain) who found that one great way to incite a move from left to right side of the brain is to duplicate a topsy-turvy line drawing. Or , to truly tally to a specific number.

Be that as it may, there are bunches of ways to actuate the move from left to
right brain thinking : Go out for a stroll in nature, go for a run, and focus on a traditional tune... even clean up yourself in shower. It's constancy of certain activities that causes the shift in Brain activities. The more we trained our muscle – which incorporates the rightside brain – the more intense and enthusiastic it turned into.

From Mark McGuinness of Lateral movement:

What's the one major goal you need to complete?

The huge danger for hyper-associated imaginative specialists is that approaching
needs and virtual diversions hinder genuine efficiency – i.e. making advances to

your enormous, unnerving, intense, and (at last) beneficial
inventively demanding circumstances. In the event that you
complete ONE huge venture these days –
one draft format, one liquidation, one photograph shoot, and one
top to bottom
practice – it feels like a completed day. But in the event that you
don't nail that
one part, it doesn't make a difference what number of little things
you complete,
you feel in your heart that it was a squandered day.

Making this inquiry, first factor is what encourages you to
concentrate, and organized.
From that point onward, the main things that can get in your way
are unfortunate
crises and make-up-reasons.

From Chris Guillebeau of The Artwork of Non-Conformity:

Why do you do that each and every day?

It's exceptionally hard to be productive in the long haul while attempting to do
what really makes a difference in your life. You'll need to "suck it up" every so
often to finish a beyond-any-doubt undertaking, yet for the "enormous rocks"
it's much simpler to develop your work around things you're excited about.

From Scott Belsky of Behance:

Is what I'm going to do advancing my goal?

Commonly, in inventive undertakings, we react on excitement rather than reason.
Shiny new gadgets and other short term interests will be inclined to deplete our
 psychological resources. Before you assign time to any mission, question your
proposed ultimate outcomes. Take a checker at your commitments in gatherings.

While you talk, would you say you are "content-producing" or basically
"commentating"? Be purposeful. All that you do or say should pass the ball ahead
 nearer to your objective. On the off chance that it doesn't, it is vulnerable to
squandering valuable power and gets you off track.

From Cal Newport of look at Hacks:

What's your training manual for expanding your ability for mindfulness
 with something, without the mind getting diverted?

This "intense focus" is at the focal point of finishing top notch work in a smaller
measure of time – be it writing a book or whatever else. Extreme brain capability
 is like a muscle that expects extreme preparing. (While helping students with this
 capability, for instance, I've had them begin with 20-minute of

undistracted work,

after which include 10 minutes consistently.)
To disregard this muscle, and thus keep on working with your email open and Facebook
 signin repeatedly, brainstorming for many excuses about why this association with
emails and facebook ,is "vital" to your procedure, makes you like the wannabe
weigh lifter who declines to hit the weight room. You're not a contender anymore.

I 'M PLANNING TO WRITE ANOTHER
EBOOK ABOUT OUR BRAIN
REGARDING FOCUS .IF YOU WOULD

LIKE A FREE COPY OF IT ,PLEASE REPLY TO MY

EMAIL ADDRESS: vikpeter83@gmail.com

ON THE SUBJECT,WRITE: "I WANT THE FREE EBOOK"
JUST MAKE SURE TO PUT MY EMAIL ADDRESS ON YOUR CONTACT LIST SO THE EBOOK WON'T END UP IN YOUR SPAM.

PLEASE LEAVE A REVIEW OF THIS BOOK ON AMAZON.WOULD APPRECIATE.THANK YOU.

RECORD

EVERYTHING DOWN

What do you record? For a large number of us, composing comprises of messages, adventure records, and maybe the standard works undertaking. In any case, setting aside a few minutes to expressly state certain things, which incorporates our every day audits, our wants, and our scholarly garbage can change the manner in which we experience our lives.

Here are six special techniques that shows, how recording things can change your reality, and what you can do to benefit from each.

1. It clears your brain for more advance thoughts.

You can clean your brain by methods of recording information in various ways.

David Allen, productiveness speaker and author, suggests doing what he calls a "center dump". This involves recording each mission, intriguing project, and undertaking you have to address. This may shift from getting milk in transit home, to a multi-individual task at work. Recording each "to-do" thing you can consider, it clears space in your mind for additional important subjects.

You can likewise utilize a system called "morning pages", which was first spearheaded by Julia Cameron, maker of The Artist's way. The "morning pages" practice involves finishing 3 pages (around 750 words) of stream-of-cognizance composing. Through doing this errand every morning, you clear your head in anticipation of the day to accomplish your greatest critical reasoning ability.

2. It encourages preparing your feelings.

Recording what's in our mind is a marvelous method to work

through inner mental clash or powerful feelings around a particular subject. It's much the same way as talking through a circumstance with a companion, it's a helpful way of fortifying your self-calming capacities and improving your self-knowledge.

3. It offers you a record for what's to come in the near future.

In the event that you keep a diary and routinely record your thinking and feelings,before long, you'll have a document of your contemplations or thinking which you may ,some way or another ,have overlooked.

Reading back through this document on your daily life ,isn't just funny—it additionally offers an important knowledge into your own thoughts procedure and important knowledge on your emotional way of life. You can acknowledge minutes moment of your life that you've most likely overlooked and develop your levels of appreciation.

Keeping a diary can likewise expand your levels of self-trust. When you may look again and perceive how proficiently you've navigated and treated critical options and entangled circumstances later on, you'll be more guaranteed of your capability to achieve future desires.

4. You advantage as a matter of fact of achievement.

Recording matters down can encourage a feeling of accomplishment and advancement, expanding our chances and developing our productiveness.

When we keep a diary of our daily life, it's unimaginably satisfying to fill at least one diaries with our contemplations and feelings. Numerous individuals harbor wants of composing a book, yet draw back at to what extent of time it takes to write a book. When you complete a diary, you'll appreciate that you have composed a book. This opens up a fresh out of the box new feel of conceivable outcomes, now not just in writing, however, but in several areas of our lives, too.

Similarly, if we have a tendency to write down everything we would like to try and do in a very specific day or week, we benefit from an extra sensation of pride once, having completed the goals, we are ready to strike the task off our list. Feeling productive enhances our productivity, making a virtuous cycle.

5. It facilitates your observation skills.

Writing things down offers you opportunity to think up huge goal and think purposefully about your goal. Regardless of what's occurring in the outside world, when we write things down, we are entering a sphere of good opportunity in life.

Doing this helps us to go through life with motivation, and it also lessen the chance of us giving in to self-destructive behaviours. But even if we do give in to self-destructive behaviours, we are going to continue writing things down so that we can understand our own emotions.

once we write things down, we've got a motivation to search our dreams and adventure that we might not otherwise experience had we not written it down . By writings things down, we have opportunity to adapt our ideas and goals to our liking.

6. It causes you to be a lot more dedicated.

Additionally to providing an area for exploring prospects, by writing our goals and endeavour , makes us feel more sure that we will achieve the goal. Like any dream or goal, they are achievable only when they're SMART: specific, measurable, actionable, realistic, and timed. These are the different stuff that we are going to learn in coaching class.

Writing down our goal is the 1st step to achieving them. It may encourage us to become more responsible. Once you've made public your goal-to-achieve , in writing, stick the writing in a place where you'll be able to see it for constant motivation.

I 'M PLANNING TO WRITE ANOTHER EBOOK ABOUT OUR BRAIN REGARDING FOCUS .IF YOU WOULD LIKE A FREE COPY OF IT ,PLEASE REPLY TO MY

EMAIL ADDRESS: vikpeter83@gmail.com

ON THE SUBJECT,WRITE: "I WANT THE FREE EBOOK"

JUST MAKE SURE TO PUT MY EMAIL ADDRESS ON YOUR CONTACT LIST SO THE EBOOK WON'T END UP IN YOUR SPAM.

PLEASE LEAVE A REVIEW OF THIS BOOK ON AMAZON.WOULD APPRECIATE.THANK YOU.

CITIZEN'S

SCRUTINY

From the beginning ,accepting public scrutiny is a good approach to moving towards your goals. Your brain has the amazing skills to speak itself out of just about any goal you want to achieve . once you have a goal you would like to accomplished, or a business you would like to start, or life amendment you would like to start , your mind would use its ability to give you wrong information to convince you why you should not be achieving your goal. Our brain are usually wired negatively in that manner, simply know it and move forward in life. That is why you should not be thinking too much if you want to achieve a goal. You should just go and do it ,because the more you think about it, the more your usually negative brain will try to talk you out of doing it.

By presenting your project or goal to the public eye , and

requesting scrutiny about the project from the public, you are telling your mind to stop chattering its negative talk. By stopping your mind to talk negatively , you are making a huge progress towards your goal.

If you have never seek public scrutiny before, the first time when you present yourself and your goal to achieve ,to the public ,you will feel uncomfortable, which is totally alright. The inconvenience feeling you felt , is actually your mind defending against your new thinking and experience. If you encircled yourself with people who support you, their support should motivate you .

We are now going to discuss personal responsibility.

Perhaps you're not engaged on a project that needs public scrutiny. perhaps you want to start changes to your private life, that you do not wish to be known on social media. Its absolutely alright as long as you seek out a scrutiny partner to scrutinize your project . When seeking your scrutiny partner, you would like to find someone who has these key characteristics:

a) They should be reliable and you should be able to contact them asap.

b) They're okay with the work of scrutinizing you.

c)They are able to relate to your goal achievement.For example, you would not choose someone who never been to a gym ,to help you build your muscle. Or you would never seek someone who

never drove a car, to help you drive one .
d)You can be frank with this person and they're going to reply with honest and open feedback.

e)A scrutiny partner can be anyone,of any profession. It can be a business partner. It can be a good friend. It can be friends of friend . It can be a facebook friend ,or an instagram friend. Whoever it might be , you must guarantee they meet the standards stated just now, so that they can really help you to achieve your goal.

Finally, I would like to say something about responsibility is that you simply may not need it on a daily basis. it's simply the motivation that keeps you going or permits you to crossover an obstacle that will inevitably appears. But, do not stop trying to find responsibility partner to scrutinized your goal ,till you have accomplished your goal. Responsibility is useful for starting your goal, however it completely is out there and accessible once you hit roadblocks that attempts to derail you from your project. You most likely won't see the obstacles coming, which is the moment when scrutiny makes all the distinction.

I 'M PLANNING TO WRITE ANOTHER EBOOK ABOUT OUR BRAIN REGARDING FOCUS .IF YOU WOULD LIKE A FREE COPY OF IT ,PLEASE REPLY TO MY

EMAIL ADDRESS: vikpeter83@gmail.com

ON THE SUBJECT,WRITE: "I WANT THE FREE EBOOK"
JUST MAKE SURE TO PUT MY EMAIL ADDRESS ON YOUR CONTACT LIST SO THE EBOOK WON'T END UP IN YOUR SPAM.

PLEASE LEAVE A REVIEW OF THIS BOOK ON AMAZON.WOULD APPRECIATE.THANK YOU

POSITIVE THINKING – DAILY RITUALS

Instead of looking for support from people, I look for positive thinking from my brain by encircling me with constant positive rituals.

Though , it seems silly when I said to myself "don't stop, keep it up, you can reach there." but, it works.

Concentration—like I said, this works on behalf of me, maybe its not be right for you, however I needed to let you know about one secret which has supported me to help me get through non stop in business success .

I have never fully understood the precise act of top quality positive chanting rituals, till one random day, when I was about twenty five years of age, that I finally understood it . Does that seems too difficult to understand that how oneday, I suddenly did understood it? Actually, doing daily positive chanting become one thing I did accidentally.

I remember when I was about nine or ten and having small very little stickers in hidden spots that expressed things like 'you go, girl' or 'fulfillment is the sum total of tiny efforts, being carried out day in and day out'. And that I remembered having mental images of the way I visualised my desired room to look like when I was twelve or sixteen, and having some serious stuff on the front of my binder with photos of however I imagine my lifestyles to be after completing my highschool. Just like a creative and discerning board.

I haven't realized at the time that presenting positive pictures where I could see, would eventually satisfied my unconscious and function as positive psychological reminders to me , whenever situations got sour, or when life routine became abnormal.

I have had some dangerous situations happened in my life. I know a number of the similar stories, but they are not mine to be told, and a few similar stories are mine own , but I rather have them stay private . However, what I'm trying to say is that : having positive reminders around the areas where I frequent, have helped my mind to stayed positive throughout the day, and prevents my mind from degenerate into daily negativity.

So , what precisely am I trying to say here ?

This is the definition of positive affirmations according to me.And you can form your own definition of positive affirmations: To have positive reminders all over the place where I frequent, that facilitate your cheerful positive life and helps you to take positive action to achieved your goal in life.

For example, a positive affirmations could suggest high selling prices of your house, burning candles and chanting positive affirmations, or your business cards on show to let you know of your dreams, a little piggy bank with a positive picture inside it, or a picture that means something very important to you , or a motivational book in amazon, or a phrase that you constantly remind yourself every morning.

My girlfriend, Jenny gave me a photo frame for my birthday with a sentences that says : You are the newest billionaires on the planet!

Every morning when I woke up, I just have to open my eyes, and look directly ahead, and there, right before of my eyes, the photo frame is hanging on the door ten feet away. Though I might have forgot to look at it someday, but I'm quite sure my subconscious mind would not have missed it !

Sometimes, Small effective existence prices are saved around my house. Some on the secret location, whereas some in open areas.

Anytime I leave my home, I can see a picture haning on the door that says " Complete Your Project." Again, perhaps we don't acknowledge it…but we see it once we arrived at our house and everytime when we depart from our house.

I do blogging patiently. From time to time I write positive chanting rituals on my blog post, and in front of the audience, so that I can look at the positive chanting rituals along with thousands of my friends. Like this publication regarding my wedding. It's get into the open currently, my meager list, however as a minimum it's a beginning, you know right? And currently I have place my ideas on Instagram to share a specific quote that resonated.

I even went so much as to hide the terrible stuff that was happening on Facebook and solely 'LIKE' post that were alright, inspirational, and encouraging. A variety of my favorites are: funny videos, pranks, e-commerce, how to make money online, self-help books, cooking recipes.

I have desired to start my own foundation, thus I created a small amount of creative and discerning board & I preserve it on show in TSC workplace.

Even my iPhone notes have marvelous positive saying! There are plenty of sayings, reminders on my iphone.

I've got great motivation all over in my life.

It's the power of positive ideas, right?

As a result of being in recovery from a bad surgery I've tried to put quite a number of positive chanting rituals everywhere in the house. I've got healing candle oils burning, turmeric in hand, clean meals easily available, soothing music, top quality folks, and being contended by reminders and books all around.

I do not permit negativity into my mind.

If this method are some stuff you are excited in discovering, then I would advise you to go looking for it. What's encompassing you ? Are you encircled with positive chanting saying all around ? If you are looking to start a business, what's your daily positive chanting rituals to help you in your business success? Are your visions and prophesy setup before you thus you'll be able to look over them? If you're going out with a family members ,or friends, Are there some prompters around to remind you of what task to carry out? If you're attempting to adjust to a healthy living, is that living method the sole one that's encompassing you? If you have got a great life goal, are there inspiration everywhere to make sure you do not forget your life goal?

DIVIDE THE WORK INTO SMALL PIECES

The truth is that ability increase when on rails.When the rails disappears time seeps into everything and slow down our motivation.

 Trellis would be preferred,thank you.

Create your, structures and process similar to a trellis. while not a trellis, your vines can't flourish within the direction you would like them to grow. A trellis permits the natural, innovative electricity to flourish, play and grow within the direction you would like it to.

Todd Henry talks regarding setting up "rails."

"It takes deliberation to move with innovative goals on noone's time, but our own time – rails don't merely build themselves." From the unintentional inventive podcast episode #143, "Rails." Multi-tasking could be a lie. Yes, a straightforward graphic might also solely take seven minutes to make, however what is it interrupting? That interruption prices you all over from 15-45 minutes reckoning on what information analysis you examine. The purpose is this: shifting between dissimilar project acts sort of a too many number of project which is cause for interruptions.

We are going to end a week's price of labor for one client in four hours. however if you break that into ten minute duties wet over the course of the week, it chow up hours and hours of inventive time. the identical is true for you. If you disagree, you're incorrect….

The only way is : batching tiny obligations. This image illustrates the quantity of interruption electronic message causes in your day. It's quite clear what permits you the foremost time to target one, innovative mission. because of the very fact that shift among responsibilities needs a minimum of quarter-hour of lost time, you will see however the primary column will rob you of all of your day.

Copied from The four Hour work week by Tim Ferris

The machine: What We Do

Allie and that i (Adam) have distinctive ways of operating (however they quite comparable). Allie LOVES pencil and paper for her daily goal list ,but I value to hold my daily goal list in on-line so that I can accessed them from all my devices.

1.Seize All Inputs

I place the entire list into Todoist and Evernote. Ideas goes into Evernote, reminders to travel Todoist. Nothing more. If I write one thing down that I want to take into consideration, I'll snap a photograph for Evernote or set a project reminder to modify the notes to digital copies.

2. Train those you're employed with

I recently supplement a signature to the bottom of my emails calling attention to people that email isn't the method to get pressing facts.

It's simply irritating with those people that don't work the identical approach as you are doing, thus you want to teach them. You will not rely on Customers or friends to scan your minds.

3. Take control of your agenda

once I'm out of town, I'm visiting be tougher to induce hold of. Same for the weekends. Same for eleven pm. There's a amount of problems that has to exist. At any given time, Jam has 10-20 customers in a very sizable amount of your time zones and with varied levels of would like. the most effective approach we will guarantee they're all happy and rocking and transferring forward is to create damn positive we're operating terribly, terribly expeditiously.

Here square measure some suggestions:

I make the most of Calendula to cut back the amount of traumatic emails to and fro. Calendula isn't the best way to do that, it's merely the one I make the most of. It integrates with Google Calendar that is that the marvel Jam's device.

I solely build weekday & weekday open for conferences. This doesn't apply to client conferences or assignment conferences, however something outside of this can be pushed into weekday or weekday.

I limit the big variety of conferences i've got per week. Calendula makes this simple.

Not everything wants in-person conferences . Phone calls have a bent to be shorter than restaurant conferences and a lot of doubtless to remain on-topic. Emails work well for obtaining tweaks and feedback and approval. Meet only when you have to, call only when you wish to and email only when you wish to. Knowing what

works and what is most useful for you and your customers can improve energy, momentum, freedom, and further innovative power.

4. Batch tiny duties

I pay AN hour each Wednesday reviewing and designing for
financials. Jam spends three hours at the beginning of each
weekday checking wherever initiatives are directed, what's
springing up over the subsequent 7-21 days . I schedule three 30
minutes parts to pander to email process.

You may see that I've already taken some routine duties that wish
to manifest and we've batched them into some precise windows.
They'll get sorted, however they don't sneak into my day.

And we have a tendency to batch our customers' tiny tasks. In
preference to planning social media photos daily for our customers,
we have a tendency to batch them into their own time every week.
If a client message us three parts of knowledge each day every
week,its alright. we have a tendency to simply put aside a small
amount of time, sooner or later per week to complete all of it.

This is valuable. It permits every client to receive concentrated,
inventive energy from us. It permits the customers to send us stuff

everytime they need to, however we do the pictures in our own
alloted time.

47

I 'M PLANNING TO WRITE ANOTHER EBOOK ABOUT OUR BRAIN REGARDING FOCUS .IF YOU WOULD LIKE A FREE COPY OF IT ,PLEASE REPLY TO MY

EMAIL ADDRESS: vikpeter83@gmail.com

ON THE SUBJECT,WRITE: "I WANT THE FREE EBOOK"
JUST MAKE SURE TO PUT MY EMAIL ADDRESS ON YOUR CONTACT LIST SO THE EBOOK WON'T END UP IN YOUR SPAM.

80/20 PERCENT RULE

Maybe you have known about the law before cause the law is uite popular, in any case, here is what is about the law.Though the law maybe applied to several areas, they especially is applied to productivity. When you keep the law in your mind while completing your project, you will gain additional time. Here is how its done:

1. economist precept

Referred to as the 80/20 rule, this is what it means : "80% of the outputs are the result of 20% of the inputs." Alfredo Pareto,an economist, coin the name, he is an Italian economic expert of nineteenth century.He started it in his Cours d'economie politique, when he realized that 80% of his nation's financial resource was

held by 20% of the citizen.

The funny thing about this law is that this law can be said to be true in many other areas , not just in the economic areas. For example, using the 80/20 percent rule or law, it can be said to be true that in any business, 80% of the profit of a business is generated by 20% of its most important clients.Or that 80% of failure is caused by

20% of most important reasons for the failure. This 80/20 rule is just a rough estimate and in many situation, the ratio of 80/20 percent rule varies a lot . For example, there maybe situation where the ratio is 90/10 percent, or 85/15 percent , or 98/2 percent .

So , if you're taking into consideration that roughly 80% of your output are the result of 20% of the input, thus it can be said that you can get the same amount of output by concentrating on 20% of the most important input, as long as you can identify correctly which are the 20% input which will give the 80% output.

By using this law accordingly, you must first identify which task would result in the most output which will result in achieving your goal much quicker. Just identify the most important task to do and focus 100% on that task only, and totally ignore the remaining unimportant task till you hae finished the most important task you have identified. After completing the most important task, now you must identify the second most important task and totally immersed yourself to complete the task, and ignore the rest till you complete the second most important task, so on and so forth.

2. Parkinson's regulation

The English student ,Cyril Northcote Parkinson, first noted that :
"Work expands with the intention to fill the time accessible in its
entireness."

Parkinson noted that, the amount of employee grew every year by
5% in the British Colony even though there are reduced paper work
every year. Therefore , a book called Parkinson's Law was printed
in 1957.

If you were employer of a company, you might have noticed this,
that if you give your employee a week to finished a project, the
employee will finished the project in one week at the minimum
even though you know that the employee could have finished the
project in three days.This is Parkinson's regulation at play here.
According the Parinson's regulation, if you set a tighter schedule to
finished the project, then the project will be done within the tight
deadlines because the tight deadlines will force you to concentrate
on the most important work which needs immediate attention, and
force you to ignore the rest of the unimportant work that does not
need immediate attention.

3. Newton's law of motion

Which is also referred to as the law of Inertia, this is the most

important law of physics developed by Isaac Newton. This law states that : "You will remain in constant motion unless you are acted upon by external unbalanced force which will change your motion direction and speed."

You can look at it this way: What is at rest remains at rest, unless acted upon by external force which will force the object to move in the direction of the force applied. And,vice versa, what is in motion remains in motion, unless acted upon by external force in the opposite direction to slow down the object in motion, or acted upon by external force in the same direction to speed up the object in motion. The point is, this law of inertia can be applied to a person. So ,according to the law, if a person is at rest, he will continue to be at rest unless the person acted upon his body into motion. And vice versa, when a person is in motion, he will continue to be in motion unless acted upon by the person to stop his body from motion to rest.

Thus keep this in mind, and obtain to figure quickly daily. Learn to require the 1st step toward finishing a task as presently as attainable. Tasks in motion tend to induce finished. thus simply begin.

STOP DOING

USELESS TASK

Once I 1st found this idea years agone, I said, "What does one mean, Marshall? I've got a lot to try and do. I've got work to attend to, dishes to clean, laundry to get done, meals to arrange, a house to scrub, and an unwell baby to take care of. None of this can joke about and that I won't have the time to look after myself, For example I won't have time to exercise, time for relaxation, or time with relatives or friends. How am I suppose to play once I've got such a lot of work duties?"

The solution is to give compassion to yourself, then you will recognised that even after lots of hard work, you must have some fun. What will Marshall Rosenberg teach regarding finding a way to have compassion for ourselves? "

An important kind of self-compassion is to create alternatives impression in easy terms via our need to create contributions to existence rather that out of concern, guilt, disgrace, or obligation. When we are motivated to help others and ourselves, even busy work should comes with some fun in it. A happy pursuit completed out of duty, obligation, worry, guilt, or disgrace can lose its pleasure and sooner or later engender resistance."

Rosenberg provides three Steps for Self -Compassion.

Write a listing. List everything you are doing that you don't suppose you have got a selection regarding, that you're thinking that you have got to try and do. you will understand what proportion of your day you spend not enjoying your life or what variety of things you have make yourself into thinking that you simply need to do it.

Select each object. whereas you're finished along with your list, acknowledge to yourself that you simply do these things as a result of your choice to do it, but not because have to do. place the phrases "I elect to . . ." before of every item on the list. once I did this, i used to be alert to having some resistance to the idea of selecting to try and do these things that isn't gratifying. I believed

"I don't like better to facilitate the children tidy their area. I must. I'm the mum. They can't bonk themselves. It's too troublesome. And mythical being can't facilitate as a result of he doesn't bonk completely." which i believed, "I don't like better to build the kids' lunches. They couldn't build a balanced lunch themselves. They don't understand how to try and do this."

Get in contact with the aim. With each object to your list, determine what your purpose at the rear of it's. Write for every object "I decide to do it simply because i would like to." Once I did this for myself I noticed that I select to help the children in tidying their area as a result of the good feeling I get once the home is clean. At the same time, it gives me an opportunity to help them maintain things so that they will improve in the future . And that I will facilitate them to study the task of improvement, by breaking things down into smaller pieces and educating them to be strategic. I yet ought to prompt myself throughout area improvement what my intention is. currently that I perceive why I'm doing it and what I worth over it, I will have some flexibility and lightness with our improvement.

WATCH OVER

YOUR PRECIOUS TIME

The most crucial requirement to time management is to protect your precious time from the unimportant stuff, so as to permit yourself to target the important goal. It's that simple. However, in actually doing it, it will be frustrating. Every now and then when you are trying to manage your time, you will make some people unhappy as you cannot make time for them, so you will be seen as a jerk, but that's ok because you are trying to adjust your time in

relation to others, and in time, everything will be adjusted.

Some people like to waste time but not you. There is a saying at Microsoft ,we use to say this when our time is wasted: randomise. I am randomised by approach of him. Please don't randomise me. If this meeting will become randomizing (time wasting), we can do the meeting over email. What a randomization! I'm not exactly sure where it came from – doubtless from losing time to a random generator – but the idea is that if there is one thing that is randomizing, it's to be prevented at all cost. I believe it's nicer than saying "you cost me precious time," particularly for people who didn't understood what the meaning of the word "Randomize."

"Do not randomized me!"

The one largest time-waster within the company is the conference meeting. Most one-hour conferences are actually 45 minutes of people hearing themselves talk and only 10 minutes are useful communication. You'll not be able to avoid the conference completely; but, you can try if you want. Actually, most of the important thing happens outside of conferences meeting rather than inside the conference. As you most have read about My Day: The method I use when I Work, Rest, and Play, my workday will easily be filled from 9 am to 7 pm if I'm not careful. This is not only applies to my situation, it applies to many people.Lots of people find themselves spending evenings and weekends to "catch up"

rather than spending the time for rest. Worse, they've make up their mind to attend the conferences.I can't make out those people whose job is solely to attend conferences – or just answer email at all times for that matter – regardless of what activities they attend... and for folk who suppose it's their activity, my wager is they're filled with guilt as a result of their negligible contributions. Regardless of what you are doing, you should maximise your contribution to the company's project. You should spend your time making and generating than eating and attending time wasting conference.You should generate big output.You should be like somebody who pushes the boulder another foot up the Hill everyday. You don't have to run in circle like everybody around you! Unless you're a full-time hole puncher with thirty years of expertise, you have one thing specific and large to give a contribution to. Useless conferences place you aloof from your work. If they're not wasting a lot time,nevertheless, they are wasting valuable opportunities to get a lot of work done.Conferences is not the place where you can make your mark. It's essential to look at conferences – together with phone calls – in terms of their worth. An example of opportunity cost is from Wikipedia: somebody who has $15 will either purchase a CD or a shirt. If he buys the shirt, the opportunity cost is the CD and if he buys the CD the opportunity cost is the shirt. Same idea applies to conferences. If you attend that 60-minute meeting, what else may you have got accomplished in that 60-minute, uninterrupted time? That output is that the opportunity cost of attending the meeting.You should make your mind up if it's worthwhile..Sometimes it is.Most of the time, it is not. What I've realized is that the majority of the 30-minute conferences can be

done over email if you can figure out the result of the meeting beforehand. Most 60-minute conferences can be completed in twenty minutes or less. very like work, conferences can fill the time allotted. If a room is set-aside for hr, the final public doesn't begin standing up till their hr are expended. It's a rare territorial issue, sort of a pride of lions protective their turf. "I'm not visiting get on my feet, it's my time!" in fact, the identical could also be expressed within the inverse – once in a very whereas, a 15-minute communique will save hr of back-and-forth through email. It takes observe to see the proper approach. Before getting in these suggestions, begin with a basic "what if" exercise. once you take a look at a gathering on your calendar, raise yourself, "What if I didn't attend this? What's the worst that might occur if I delegated, cancelled, or declined the meeting?" square measure you comfy with the expected outcome? If thus, don't move – evoke the notes or a quick verbal précis as presently because the meeting is over. just in case you continue to sense you would like to be there, raise yourself, "What might I do to decrease the impact of not attending?" now and again, this includes writing a quick paragraph to stipulate your angle and what you hope to induce out of the time. offer folks time to reply over email 1st, and you'll be able to avoid the meeting altogether. If you continue to wish to fulfill, you will a minimum of be capable of shortening the time you would like to pay.

Here are some established ways in which to

save lots of some time:

1. Get a schedule before agreeing to meetings with everyone. coming into a space to stipulate AN agenda could be a waste of your time. Conferences have to be regarding problem-solving, not deciding what's wrong – that should occur before of the meeting. There square measure many instances wherever you'll be able to check the timetable and convey the identical final results while not the meeting. I've began to use a handy model for conferences (apologies before just in case you've been one in every of the recipients): "Will you send over AN agenda for the meeting thus we have a tendency to square measure ready to build the foremost of the time? i would like to create positive I'm organized, thus please let American state grasp wish you'd prefer to cowl and the way I'm ready to assist." Word of caution: now and again folks take offense to the present. However, it's dead acceptable to ask folks to replicate on however they're visiting use their time before they are doing. you have got different matters you may be doing, as I'm bound they are doing too. after they send the schedule over, you'll be able to decide if the time is basically needed.

2.Advocate a brand new time for all conferences which could be set for AN hour

AN hour could be a very long time. It will ruin your workday, take up your lunch, different conferences, and slash it slow such a lot that you simply solely get 2 or 3 hours each day to induce stuff done. If you are doing too several hour-long conferences, you're visiting be one in every of these folks repining that they don't have time to try and do their job. As mentioned earlier, many folks can fill the scheduled hour because of the very fact they suppose they need to – in the end, it's on the calendar. Use time as a forcing perform – schedule it for abundant less time than you're thinking that it should take and see if you'll be able to bonk. Here's however I usually approach this: "My day is slammed with conferences and completely different commitments. Let's see if we will do this in twenty minutes – I promise to air time – and if we are going to not get wise completed, we will forever follow-up over email or schedule another fast set. Would ten to 10:20 am work for you? If not, I'm conjointly free from three to 3:20 or 4:40 to 5. Thanks!" The word of caution from higher than applies here too I remember the primary time someone did this to American state years agone, I felt unhappy. I got over it the minute i noticed I had to try and do it too. Expect others to moreover. Your whole organization will discover ways in which to figure smarter.

3.Batch conferences jointly in order that you have got time to complete actual work

to try and do what you would like to, you would like devoted, non-stop time. Time to induce ramped up, and time to complete. Innovative work is tough and isn't typically dead in 10-minute periods. It will take half-hour simply to work out what you're visiting do each currently and so. the answer to this: keep non-stop blocks of your time special daily. This involves providing new times for conferences others have founded and taking an in depth take a look at your calendar before setting up place a gathering to start out with. that day does one suppose would be additional effective? {consider|think regarding|contemplate|take into account} what proportion you may get done just by being proactive about this.

4. founded short standing conferences as instead of sitting conferences.

It's superb how briskly conferences go once you can't get relaxed in a very seat. On each occasion I will avoid it, I don't schedule sitting conferences. once you're standing, you're perpetually asking yourself "why am I standing here?" and also the inducement to require a seat will assist in pushing the meeting on. It's funny looking at understand this in a very meeting. on the identical lines, you will schedule your standing conferences in a very tiny, incommodious house in preference to a spacious convention area stuffed with snacks and projectors. Use a person's workplace or a shared open house rather than a vicinity wherever people's merely "settle in and obtain comfy". I'll take a 15-minute standing meeting in a very tiny workplace over a 60-minute sitting meeting in a very room any day.

5.Avoid routine conferences (without a transparent schedule). Routine conferences have three states in my experience:

They recur timely (~50% of them) They recur too late (~40% of them) They recur simply at the proper time (~10% of them) generally, regular conferences square measure simply ways in which to book time on people's calendars in order that you'll be able to get them jointly. plenty of your time, a minimum of at Microsoft. If you are trying to book AN ad-hoc meeting, nobody will attend as a result of they need different conferences already scheduled . Routine conferences preserve that time on their calendars set-aside just for you. Most of those routine conferences either recur timely (nothing to speak about) or too late (you need to have already met – and sometimes have). reckoning on wherever you're employed, you will not be ready to get out of all standard conferences – but, you'll be able to {try to|attempt to|try ANd} guarantee there's an agenda sent before time, or that they're performed {in a|during a|in an exceedingly|in a terribly} tiny space at the very least, and you will quietly excuse yourself if you don't realize the meeting helpful.

6. Kill several birds with one stone

7.

I've scheduled conferences within the course of your time I had scheduled to square away my work or stroll to the business workplace. I've scheduled conferences over lunch and travel times, even selecting folks up at their house to own a gathering whereas driving to figure. I've scheduled conferences in a very racquetball court or at different social events. Humans typically acknowledge that everybody's busy. What's the distinction once the meeting takes place farewell as we're each dedicated to the ultimate results? As mentioned antecedently, i favor to mix a minimum of 1 meeting daily with a brief stroll outdoors. we have a tendency to exercise our bodies at the identical time as our brains, which ends up in additional engaged, inventive communication. conferences that serve a twin purpose will clearly build a distinction for your agenda. As another to having 1:1 conferences with people, get some folks along at a time to stay the effort of passing the results on among the organization to a minimum.

7. Cut back back-and-forth responses over email.

Now and again 2-word responses to emails will merely invite a back-and-forth exchange. "No" is by no suggests that as appropriate as "No" and here's a pair of sentences why not. E-mail isn't instant electronic communication. It's meant to be

"asynchronous", not period. usually somebody can solicit from me a yes/no question through email that I should simply simply respond with one word. Of course, if I'm capable of assume their response, or if i do know their motivation ab initio, a small amount a lot of written in a very single e-mail will facilitate U.S.A. lower the back-and-forth. As AN example: "Yes, that's the approach the merchandise is meant. we have a tendency to set to try and do it this fashion because of the very fact the data we've gathered indicates that individuals use this choice in zero.05% of client categories. For additional facts on the precise implementation info and actual justification, you should take a glance at out the specifications (right here's the link). when viewing this, if you continue to have queries, please be happy to email. convey you!" this is applicable to setting up place time to induce along moreover. spoken language "I'm free at four" isn't as powerful as "I'm free at four. If you're not free at four, does you wish to provide alternatives so I will select the most appropriate time for us?" you'll be able to save a minimum of 3 emails that approach.

8. Get out of the habit of responding to your phone once it rings

Reply {to all|to all or ANy|to any or all} phone calls with an email or text thus you'll be able to work whereas you would like. a decent response to AN unmarked voicemail could also be one thing similar to the subsequent – apothegmatic while not wiggle room: "Hi Bob, I detected that you referred to as American state. Sorry I wasn't accessible. If that's regarding the issue on Friday, I'm presently set-aside on AK flight 416 and conceive to get to the aerodrome at 3:30. I'll forestall to seeing you at the gate which I'll have the files we have a tendency to mentioned. See then you – pls. email American state if you have got any queries. Thanks!" Unless it's a member of my family or an in depth friend, I don't answer my phone if I'm within the middle of one thing. My voicemail asks folks to send American state a text or AN email as critical going away a voicemail (which takes time to concentrate on). however if they are doing leave a voicemail, I forever follow-up with email or text. It forces folks (including me) to be apothegmatic, and keeps U.S.A. from having to be accessible at the identical time.

FINAL ANALYSIS

Is your character that if an efficient person? Have you ever questioned what makes one person more efficient than the other person? In contrast to what people may think, being effective is not only about one's mind or capability. Being effective is also about using good effective habits over other ineffective habits, so as to get the most from your time. As somebody very curious about private productivity, i've got found eight habits to be superior in boosting one's effectiveness in time management. Use them and watch your productivity rocket to the moon!

Daily Habit 1: Leave no bones unturn in finding and cancelling the unimportant task. The most important habit of a efficient humans is to cut and cut and chop your schedule till you're solely left with only and only what is the most important task or project or goal. For everything you're doing currently, question yourself the importance of the task. Will this bring you toward your dream or goals? Will this produce any real impact on your life in the long term? Is it absolutely the best way to use your time, or might you be doing some other higher-value tasks or doing something more important ? If the answer is 'yes' to any or all of those queries, keep this work. If not, probably it's time to remove the task. No real purpose in doing a task or work which does not bring you towards your goal! Say you're handling a project that creates no difference to your business when it's completed. It doesn't matter whether or not you take an hour, 3 hours, or one week to try and do it—it still won't create any difference at the end of the day! Many folks tend to incorrectly think everyday duties as high responsibilities. A terrific tool to line them aside is the Time management Matrix that classifies our daily activities into four special quadrants. Your most important obligations fall beneath Quadrant 2, that ought to be your quadrant of focus.

Daily Habit 2: Schedule breaks from your work strategically. I don't suppose being effective necessitate you to work non-stop like a machine.Infact, working non-stop will cause you to become less productive as you will run out of energy. whereas the amount of hours spent on work will increase and also the quantity of work performed seems slightly higher, the work completed per unit of your time is less than your average. Thus while it looks as if you're doing a lot of work, in reality, you're not. In economic science study, this is referred to as the Law of Diminishing Returns.

It is important to schedule time for rest. Regardless of how much you want to work, there are areas of your life that working at your project can't fulfill, your work cannot fulfill love, family, fitness. That's why our life-style wheel is created from varied segments, vs. merely one massive 'work' phase. Every phase is different and cannot be replaced by others. By "relaxation", I mean scheduling time for any section of your existence that's outside of business/career/research. Scheduling a break from work charges your batteries ,in order that you'll be able to charge ahead forward once you come back to the task at hand.

If you're a freelance or on a flexible work schedule,you can use this method easily. whether or not you're in a very 9-5 workplace setting, you'll be able to practice it . Whenever you're feeling

unproductive, add a quick break. Walk off from your workdesk, get a drink from the canteen, move for a rest room break, or sit down and chat with a colleague about anything. You'll be refilled with much energy once you come back from your break.

Daily Habit 3: Remove your productivity pit stops (i.e.,

distractions) Productivity pit stops reduce your productivity. They could be the music you are playing while you are working, they could be your slow pc, unnecessary phone calls, notifications from your inbox regarding incoming messages, the wifi, instagram, Pinterest, YouTube, Facebook, Twitter, and lots of others.These things traps you and prevent you from getting your important task done. Watch your own habits everyday and notice whenever your work decrease. What exactly is distracting you from your important work ahead? Watch how you work in particular locations and ,accordingly, Change your surroundings to a better work friendly location. Do adjustments here and there.As much productivity pit stops you can discover and remove,the more effective you'll be.

Habit 4: Look into your ideas, how does one do this? Easy, consider what you would like out of life. Is it letting others develop? Connecting with humans? Being recognized for your work? Getting out of poverty? serving to the unlucky? Become #1 in your field? How are you reaching them? Find out what is your motivation, and so use the motivation to force yourself into reaching your goals. My dream is to help others attain their highest capability and living good lives. I really like watching completely people living to their dreams, and if there's something preventing them I'll do everything I can to remove the prevention,thus I use this to force me in everything I try to build. If I'm writing a blog post, I'll begin through questioning what is the issue that people are having, then I channel that power.

Daily Habit 5: Build obstacles to entry .A big thing regarding our world nowadays is that it's less complicated than ever to connect with anybody. Everyone are just a text/telephone call/email/Facebook message away. But, it also causes huge distractions. Every minutes, there's a distraction coming back in, whether or not via call, text, an email, or a Facebook invite. Actually, to get any work done, you must shutoff all contact to the outside world. Disconnect your iphone, shut your inbox, set a

private rule regarding when to answer emails. I'm not suggesting that you to totally cut off from the outside world, however, you must do some of these in some ways, particularly when you're engaged on a crucial task. As time goes by, the outside world will get accustomed to your schedule and they will respect your schedule so that they can reach you.

Daily Habit 6: Take advantage of your time pockets .You usually get time pockets when you are waiting for someone, when you're commuting, when you're walking from one place to another place, etc. Check your schedule. How can you better take advantage of the time pockets? You must have somethings ready to do to take advantage of a pocket of time, like taking note of podcasts, reading books, etc. You'll be stunned at what amount of work can be done in a few minutes!

Daily Habit 7: Setting timelines ,which is one of the most

important productivity habit. According to Parkinson's Law, work expands so as to fill the time alloted for its completion -

This suggests that if you don't set a timeline or more accurately, if you do not set a deadline for the completion of the work, it will take you much longer to complete what you're doing.

If you set a timeline of one month, you'll take one month to complete the work,even though you could have completed earlier. If you set deadline of one week to complete the same work, then most probably you'll complete the work by the end of the week. And actually, if you set the deadline as one hour to complete the work, you sincerely can get the work done in one hour, if you absolutely have to, especially, say if you were forced to get the work done in one hour at gunpoint. Thus, to get any work done in time, you must set timelines or deadline.Once you set deadlines, try your best to complete the work within the deadline.

Daily Habit 8: Try to automate everything as much as possible. Nowaday, automation is feasible for lots of things. Whether or not it's not possible to completely automate everything, we can still use the automation systems to get many work done.

I 'M PLANNING TO WRITE ANOTHER EBOOK ABOUT OUR BRAIN REGARDING FOCUS .IF YOU WOULD LIKE A FREE COPY OF IT ,PLEASE REPLY TO MY

EMAIL ADDRESS: <u>vikpeter83@gmail.com</u>

ON THE SUBJECT,WRITE: "I WANT THE FREE EBOOK"
JUST MAKE SURE TO PUT MY EMAIL ADDRESS ON YOUR CONTACT LIST SO THE EBOOK WON'T END UP IN YOUR SPAM.

PLEASE LEAVE A REVIEW OF THIS BOOK ON AMAZON.WOULD APPRECIATE.THANK YOU

TO BE NOTED

No a part of the information contain within can be duplicated, place away for future use, or transfer in any ways, electronic, mechanical, photocopied, recorded, filtered, or the rest, apart from as allowed under U.S copyright law, without the written permission of the author.

85

www.ingramcontent.com/pod-product-compliance
Lightning Source LLC
Chambersburg PA
CBHW072203170526
45158CB00004BB/1748